# 2,001 Things to Do
# Before You Die

# 2,001 Things to Do Before You Die

## by Dane Sherwood

**A Stonesong Press Book**

HarperPerennial
*A Division of HarperCollinsPublishers*

HarperCollins books may be purchased for educational, business, or sales promotional use. For information, please write
to: Special Markets Department, HarperCollins Publishers,
Inc., 10 East 53rd Street, New York, New York 10022.

Book design and typography by Steven Rosen

**FIRST EDITION**

A Stonesong Press Book

Library of Congress Cataloging-in-Publication Data
Sherwood, Dane.
    2,001 things to do before you die / Dane Sherwood. — 1st ed.
        p.     cm.
    ISBN 0-06-273490-3
    1. Conduct of life—Miscellanea.     I. Title.
  BJ1595.S453   1997
  248.4—dc21                                          96-39971

97 98 99 00 01 ❖/HC 10 9 8 7 6 5 4 3 2 1

# Acknowledgments

The author is indebted to the following people for their contributions to the book:

The Ackers, Amanda Beeler, Jan "H-Man" Beran, Sheree Bykofsky, Michele Camardella, Scott Carson, Steven Cook, Irving Fieldstadt, Jennifer Gauthier, Dr. Irving Gerstman, DDS, everyone from HarperCollins who contributed, Representative Rachel Kaprielian, Elizabeth and Douglas Lancaster, Brigid Mellon, Janet Rosen, Dawn Sangrey, Vincent Scialla, Sven Slopenhagen, Burt Solomon, Jessica Wolk-Stanley, Pinky Tuscadero, Barbie, Spud, Ya Hooverville, and Daisy.

An extra special thanks to Kerry Acker, Alison Fargis Beran, Paul Fargis, Michele Farbman, Rob Kaplan, Steven Rosen, and Nick Viorst. I couldn't have done it without you.

*Imagine. You've just learned that planet Earth will explode in six months. Or, a virulent parasite is wiping out the chimp population and it's beginning to strike humans—it's sure to be the worst plague in the history of humankind. What ever will you do during your last days on Earth?*

Surely you've considered this scenario before. Who hasn't? Just what things should, could, or would you do if you knew your days on this planet were numbered?

Then again, maybe you have years to go. There's so much to see, to learn, to give, to do. Where to begin?

Well, here's where. *2,001 Things to Do Before You Die* is your fresh start. These ideas range from simple tasks to silly pranks, from charitable deeds to risky feats, from sweeping lifestyle changes to dramatic philosophical transformations, from the mundane to the sublime to the ridiculous.

Some of these ideas are easily achieved, others—or so the cynics will say—are nearly impossible to attain. But it is hoped that this list will inspire you to act, and—yes—to dream. Let it provoke you and prod you. Maybe it will even scare you into action. But for God's sake, use it to get off of your sorry butt and do something!

Feel free to check off the entries as you complete them. Of course, exercise your best judgment when picking and choosing which ideas to follow. There are some occasions in life where being careful is a very good idea.

There are some blank spaces at the end of this list for you to add your own ideas. If you come up with anything particularly brilliant, why don't you send it on to The Stonesong Press, 11 East 47th Street, NY, NY 10017? Who knows, maybe the only thing you do will be to get your contribution in the next printing.

So, come on. Plunge in. Do something wonderful, ridiculous, crazy, or inspiring.

What are you waiting for?

- ☐ Be an extra in a movie
- ☐ Learn the first five Amendments
- ☐ See a green iceberg
- ☐ See the aurora borealis from Denali
- ☐ Travel at warp speed
- ☐ Have dim sum for breakfast
- ☐ Milk a cow
- ☐ Donate some body parts
- ☐ Become an eccentric billionaire and run for president
- ☐ Rent an apartment on the Seine for two months
- ☐ Catch a foul ball at a professional baseball game
- ☐ Spelunk

- [ ] Win the Palme d'Or at Cannes
- [ ] Have multiple orgasms
- [ ] Drink a mint julep at the Kentucky Derby
- [ ] Pay for the next car at the toll booth
- [ ] Memorize Hamlet's "What a piece of work is man" speech
- [ ] Skywrite a message to someone
- [ ] Reconstruct a dinosaur
- [ ] Pay off your school loans
- [ ] Organize a food drive for the needy
- [ ] Have your ancestors' names engraved on the plaque at Ellis Island
- [ ] Get married at Cinderella's Castle at Disney World

> *I invent nothing. I rediscover.*
>
> *—Auguste Rodin*

☐ Make a religious pilgrimage—to Mecca, Santiago de Compostela, Jerusalem, or Graceland

☐ Master the pregnant pause and a dead-pan delivery

☐ Be a riot grrrl

☐ Change your name to have all the letters in lowercase

☐ Flirt

☐ Score a period hat trick

☐ Pay your parents back for college

☐ Read Joyce's *Ulysses* without a trot

- ☐ Hang-glide in Chamonix
- ☐ Have pizza the way it was made in Bronx bars in the 1940s
- ☐ Watch the sun set on Santoríni ☀
- ☐ Shake hands with someone famous
- ☐ Light a candle in the Holocaust Memorial Museum's Hall of Remembrance
- ☐ Swim in each of the Seven Seas
- ☐ Learn to drive a stick shift
- ☐ Master the art of letter-writing
- ☐ Record a duet with Frank Sinatra
- ☐ Throw your panties at Tom Jones
- ☐ Crush a beer can with one hand
- ☐ Blow smoke rings

- [ ] Be able to explain Einstein's theory of relativity

- [ ] Get a professional makeover

- [ ] Awake to the sounds of macaws or spider monkeys in a tropical rain forest

- [ ] Suddenly decide on and leave for a trip

- [ ] Crash a ritzy party

- [ ] Stay in bed all day

- [ ] Do something scandalous

- [ ] Testify before Congress

- [ ] Give someone a reason to believe in God

- [ ] Lobby

- [ ] Participate in a moonlit drum circle

- [ ] Start a Barbie collection
- [ ] Create a zine
- [ ] Build a tree house
- [ ] Attend a *Star Trek* convention
- [ ] Write a letter to the editor
- [ ] Swim in Icelandic hot springs at sundown
- [ ] Discover a new talent
- [ ] Découpage a table
- [ ] Communicate without words
- [ ] Eat alligator
- [ ] Spend one month completely alone
- [ ] Spend one month without a car
- [ ] Spend one month without a television

> *We are what we pretend to be.*
>
> —*Kurt Vonnegut, Jr.*

☐ Spend one month without a radio

☐ Spend a day at a nursing home

☐ Play hide and seek with your partner

☐ Do an open-mike night

☐ Approach a stranger and ask him/her out

☐ Clean out your closet and give your throwaway clothes and shoes to the poor

☐ Donate books

☐ Interview your friends on video camera

- [ ] Interview yourself on video camera
- [ ] Take a natural mud bath
- [ ] Read to children
- [ ] Listen to Mozart's Requiem without interruption
- [ ] Read *Atlas Shrugged*
- [ ] Give a taxi driver some advice
- [ ] Write your high school teacher a thank-you note
- [ ] Leave some cookies in your mailbox for the mailman
- [ ] Become familiar with duende
- [ ] Find the perfect Peking duck
- [ ] Wake up next to Brad Pitt or Michelle Pfeiffer

- ☐ Take an acting class

- ☐ Be a docent in a museum

- ☐ Ski Tuckerman's Ravine

- ☐ Fossil-hunt

- ☐ Find a long, straight road and see how fast you can go

- ☐ Learn French, German, or Swahili

- ☐ Pogo-stick with children

- ☐ Unicycle

- ☐ Ride an ostrich

- ☐ Spend a day with a toddler

- ☐ Volunteer at the monkey house at the zoo

- ☐ Ride the Coney Island Cyclone three times in a row

- [ ] Protect the innocent
- [ ] Paint polka dots on your sneakers
- [ ] Experience 1000 types of love
- [ ] Dry some flowers
- [ ] Have a tremendous, rollicking, soaking-wet, water pistol fight
- [ ] Prepare a seven-course meal for ten of your closest friends
- [ ] Compete in the eco-challenge
- [ ] Scuba dive in the waters of Micronesia
- [ ] Go on a silent retreat
- [ ] Busk (perform for money) in a European country
- [ ] Ride in a dune buggy

- ☐ Attend a Democratic or Republican convention

- ☐ Protest at a Democratic or Republican convention

- ☐ Start a new political party

> *Dying seems less sad than having lived too little.*
>
> *—Gloria Steinem*

- ☐ Crochet or knit a sweater

- ☐ Travel alone

- ☐ Parasail

- ☐ Bungee-jump off a bridge

Do I contradict myself?
Very well then,
I contradict myself.
I am large,
I contain multitudes.

—Walt Whitman

- [ ] Finish a marathon (without throwing up)

- [ ] Horseback-ride on a Costa Rican beach at dawn, clothing optional

- [ ] Be the captain of a ship, a spaceship, or a submarine

- [ ] Go on a scientific expedition

- [ ] Teach someone to read

- [ ] Learn to sew

- [ ] Make your own bread

- [ ] Shoot a crossbow

- [ ] Read, understand, and memorize three poems

- [ ] Learn a new computer program

- [ ] Swallow a goldfish

- ☐ Own a velvet Elvis
- ☐ Create an unforgettable ad campaign
- ☐ Attend the Olympics
- ☐ Go paintballing
- ☐ Leave someone a $100 tip
- ☐ Hot-air balloon over a desert
- ☐ Do Outward Bound
- ☐ Haggle . . . and win
- ☐ Invent or patent something
- ☐ Press some flowers
- ☐ Cut a demo tape at a recording studio
- ☐ Skinny-dip

- [ ] Go down the Snake River in a dory

- [ ] Fill a time capsule with magazines, CDs, photographs, letters, and T-shirts, then bury it

> *Thank you, God, for this good life and forgive us if we do not live it enough.*
>
> *—Garrison Keillor*

- [ ] Ride a boxcar for a couple of days

- [ ] Bake a rhubarb pie from scratch

- [ ] Learn to play an instrument

- [ ] Venture cross-country on a Harley

- [ ] Ride a bicycle built for two

☐ Catch fireflies

☐ Visit a monastery

☐ Learn to sail

☐ Visit a synagogue

☐ Attend a Catholic Mass

☐ Meditate with monks

☐ Fast for three days (just bread and water)

☐ Attend a Unitarian Universalist service

☐ Win a Kewpie doll

☐ See the Great Wall of China

☐ Actually listen to a Jehovah's Witness

☐ Swim with dolphins

☐ Get your photo taken in Katmandu

- [ ] Do a backflip on a trampoline
- [ ] Sea-kayak
- [ ] Run with the bulls in Pamplona
- [ ] Volunteer at a national park
- [ ] Paint your bedroom red, black, or hot pink
- [ ] Watch the Cartoon Network for twenty-four hours
- [ ] Spend some time with the Amish or the Mennonites
- [ ] Read *Invisible Man*
- [ ] Build a table
- [ ] Read *Alice in Wonderland* aloud
- [ ] Ride Space Mountain
- [ ] See a laser light show at a planetarium

- [ ] Prepare a lobster dinner
- [ ] Read Dante's *Inferno*
- [ ] Make your own ice cream

> *Think excitement, talk excitement, act out excitement and you are bound to become an excited person. Life will take on a new zest, deeper interest and greater meaning.*
>
> —Norman Vincent Peale

- [ ] Watch *Spinal Tap*
- [ ] Invent an identity
- [ ] Learn to say the alphabet backward

- [ ] Spend some time in a third-world country

- [ ] Surf

- [ ] Sit in a skybox at a sporting event

- [ ] Catch the bouquet

- [ ] Spend some time in Appalachia

- [ ] Roll your own sushi

- [ ] Dance in the gazebo while on *The Sound of Music* tour in Salzburg

- [ ] Ice-skate by candlelight at midnight

- [ ] Stay at a Spanish parador

- [ ] Bathe in the Ganges

- [ ] Sit in first class

- [ ] Have a truly amazing one-night stand

THERE IS NO DESIRE
SO DEEP AS THE SIMPLE
DESIRE FOR
COMPANIONSHIP.

—GRAHAM GREENE

- [ ] Bottle your own preserves
- [ ] Become a Monty Python expert
- [ ] Buy a $100 bottle of wine and share it with your oldest friends
- [ ] Grow a beard
- [ ] Shave off your beard
- [ ] Ski by torchlight
- [ ] Provoke
- [ ] Have a local restaurant deliver breakfast in bed for two
- [ ] Hire a violinist to play while you and a loved one have dinner
- [ ] Send someone a "just thinking of you" card
- [ ] Read *Lady Chatterley's Lover*

☐ Have your palm or
   tarot cards read

☐ Walk on the beach in winter

☐ Grow an amaryllis

☐ Don't shave for a few days

☐ Order yourself a birthday cake

---

> *Half my life is an act of revision.*
>
> —*John Irving*

---

☐ Smoke a big fat cigar

☐ Rearrange all the furniture in your living room

☐ Stomp grapes in Tuscany

☐ Leave your umbrella and take a walk in the summer rain

☐ Have a designer create your personal stationery

☐ Have someone else clean your place from top to bottom

☐ Call a radio station and dedicate a song to your mom

☐ Take a bateau ride on the Seine

☐ Go someplace where you will see a moose, a bear, or a golden eagle in the wild

☐ Shoot the rapids

☐ Be the guest of honor at your own party

- [ ] Build a birdhouse
- [ ] Talk a cop out of a ticket
- [ ] Mosh
- [ ] Watch a baby being born
- [ ] Go to a religious revival
- [ ] Boogie-board
- [ ] Indulge your most private fantasy
- [ ] Wear a fez, turban, or fedora
- [ ] Trek the Himalayas with a Sherpa
- [ ] Dress up like Santa Claus and play it to the hilt
- [ ] Read or listen closely to "I Have a Dream"
- [ ] Perform a citizen's arrest

- ☐ Memorize the Gettysburg Address
- ☐ Vote
- ☐ See a bullfight
- ☐ Rethink your stance on abortion
- ☐ Find out what auld lang syne really means
- ☐ Plan the perfect April Fools' Day prank
- ☐ Become a Scrabble champ
- ☐ Win an argument
- ☐ Let someone else win an argument
- ☐ Adopt a kitten, a skunk, or a greyhound
- ☐ Try on your partner's clothes
- ☐ Drive a Maserati

 ☐ Call your mother

☐ Get call waiting

☐ Get rid of call waiting

> *If you think you can, you can.*
> *And if you think you can't, you're*
> *right.*
>
> —*Mary Kay Ash*

- ☐ Learn the names of ten constellations
- ☐ Have a bowl of Sugar Corn Pops or Peanut Butter Cap'n Crunch
- ☐ Buy a star and have it named for someone
- ☐ Ride an elephant
- ☐ Write your own *National Enquirer* article
- ☐ Plant a tree
- ☐ Get your hair cornrowed

Life is what happens to you while you're busy making other plans.

—John Lennon

- [ ] Make your own beer
- [ ] Dye your hair
- [ ] Be the protagonist of your life
- [ ] Throw a coin in the Fontana di Trevi in Rome
- [ ] Finish your dissertation
- [ ] Ride a gondola in Venice
- [ ] See a live performance of Beethoven's Ninth Symphony
- [ ] Take a helicopter ride over New York City
- [ ] Go wine-tasting in Sonoma County, California
- [ ] Change your first name
- [ ] Clean up your room

☐ Roast marshmallows in your backyard

☐ Go to an Italian opera

☐ Learn sign language

☐ Make paper dolls

☐ Fly a kite

☐ Swallow your pride

☐ Visit Ayers Rock in Australia

---

*In the end, everything is a gag.*

—Charlie Chaplin

---

☐ Toast your father for no particular reason

☐ Spend a week at a spa

- [ ] Kiss the Blarney Stone

- [ ] Sing and dance with gypsies

- [ ] Take the last train to Clarksville

- [ ] Pick, then bob for apples

- [ ] Clam with your feet

- [ ] Learn the names of ten plants that grow in the wild, and be able to identify them

- [ ] Forage—eat nothing but food grown in the wild—for one weekend

- [ ] Inspire someone

- [ ] Meet, and really speak to, three genuine eccentrics

- [ ] Send everyone you know a valentine

- [ ] Make a giant chocolate chip cookie

- [ ] Give a rousing or moving speech

- [ ] Go night-swimming in a light rain

- [ ] Watch a drive-in movie naked

- [ ] Learn a new word every day for a whole summer

- [ ] Memorize the name of the play *The Persecution and Assassination of Jean-Paul Marat as Performed by the Inmates of the Asylum at Charenton under the Direction of the Marquis de Sade*

- [ ] Watch kittens being born

- [ ] Scream as loud as you can

- [ ] Memorize "Who's On First"

The only people for me are
the mad ones, the ones who are
mad to live, mad to talk,
mad to be saved, desirous of everything
at the same time,
the ones who never yawn
or say a commonplace thing,
but burn, burn, burn like fabulous
yellow roman candles exploding.

—Jack Kerouac

☐ Question your sexuality

☐ Question your faith

☐ Question your values

☐ Question your lawyer

- [ ] Renew your vows

- [ ] Drive a bus

- [ ] Write to an athlete, writer, celebrity, or political figure you particularly admire

> *The aim of life is to live, and to live means to be aware, joyously, drunkenly, serenely, divinely aware.*
>
> —Henry Miller

- [ ] Run the Boston Marathon

- [ ] Ride a camel in the Negev Desert

- [ ] Sketch the ocean on a deserted beach

- [ ] Pilot a Lear Jet

- ☐ Plan an entire solo weekend
- ☐ Compose a steamy love letter
- ☐ Give someone a pedicure
- ☐ Play a game of Strip Monopoly
- ☐ Restore an old house
- ☐ Rent and operate a bulldozer
- ☐ Quit smoking
- ☐ Consult a plastic surgeon
- ☐ Have bookcases built in
- ☐ Get remarried
- ☐ Impress the boss
- ☐ Make chocolate chip pancakes
- ☐ Stay at Balmer's Herberge in Switzerland

- [ ] Line dance or hand-jive
- [ ] Be frivolous
- [ ] Travel the globe
- [ ] Interview your grandparents about their childhoods
- [ ] Research your family tree
- [ ] Invest in the stockmarket
- [ ] Write a haiku
- [ ] Speak in haiku
- [ ] Train a seeing-eye dog
- [ ] Learn the second stanza of "The Star Spangled Banner"
- [ ] Plan a picnic for one
- [ ] Predict the next big thing

- [ ] Win an Olympic medal
- [ ] Write a great novel
- [ ] Live in Tangiers
- [ ] Have a house on the ocean
- [ ] Be a star
- [ ] Retire young
- [ ] Have a long, warm, serious talk with your folks
- [ ] Win a trophy
- [ ] Sing the "Hallelujah" chorus in the shower
- [ ] Be an expert witness
- [ ] Mediate a dispute
- [ ] Perfect your yodel

- [ ] Change jobs
- [ ] Plead innocent to a speeding ticket
- [ ] Mend fences
- [ ] Memorize all the dialogue of your favorite movie
- [ ] Master auto mechanics
- [ ] Love more than once
- [ ] Snowmobile
- [ ] Dance with glee
- [ ] Invite your employees home for dinner
- [ ] Write your memoirs

> *I'm not going to die wondering.*
>
> *—Colette*

> *Hope for the best. Expect the worst. Life is a play. We're unrehearsed.*
>
> —Mel Brooks

- [ ] Take a Chinese cooking class
- [ ] Pierce something on your body
- [ ] Get a tattoo
- [ ] Remove your tattoo
- [ ] Achieve washboard abs
- [ ] Slide down a banister
- [ ] Live beyond your means
- [ ] Witness a miracle
- [ ] Splurge at Tiffany's

- ☐ Race in the Iditarod
- ☐ Rent a Virgin Island
- ☐ Attend a Hollywood premier
- ☐ Quarterback for the Dallas Cowboys
- ☐ Be a Dallas Cowboy's Cheerleader
- ☐ Surf the Net
- ☐ Spend a weekend at the Waldorf-Astoria in New York City
- ☐ Box
- ☐ Solve a mystery
- ☐ Have a signature color
- ☐ Have a Halloween bonfire with hot apple cider
- ☐ Design a garden

- [ ] Memorize the prologue of Chaucer's *Canterbury Tales* in Middle English
- [ ] Keep track of love
- [ ] Write your own vows
- [ ] Hike the entire Appalachian Trail
- [ ] Take a wine-tasting course
- [ ] Be the "It" girl of your generation
- [ ] Sew a quilt
- [ ] Rediscover your lover's body
- [ ] Attend a school reunion
- [ ] Run for office
- [ ] Shave your head
- [ ] Eat a vegamite sandwich
- [ ] Write your name in wet cement

- [ ] Learn to play Beethoven's *Emperor* Concerto
- [ ] Conduct a symphony orchestra
- [ ] Be the Grand Marshal in a St. Patrick's Day Parade

> *God help those who do not help themselves.*
>
> —*Wilson Mizner*

- [ ] Win an election
- [ ] Chair a board
- [ ] Write a play
- [ ] Dance at your grandchild's wedding

- [ ] Dance at your great-grandchild's wedding
- [ ] Learn to eat rice with chopsticks
- [ ] Learn to whistle with two fingers
- [ ] Make the perfect soufflé
- [ ] Rescue someone
- [ ] Make angels in the snow
- [ ] Watch a hummingbird
- [ ] Walk an elderly person across the street
- [ ] Bicycle through Amsterdam
- [ ] Take a milk bath
- [ ] Burn sandalwood incense
- [ ] Play with puppies

☐ Bare your soul to a stranger

☐ Debate deconstructionism, Sartre, objectivism, and the definition of art, preferaby in a smoky cafe

☐ Drink mulled wine on a snowy night in Prague

☐ Create your own comic strip

☐ Lie naked on a wide open field beneath a brilliant moon

☐ Record your dreams

☐ Make a photo album or collage for your best friend

- ☐ Travel by bus in Central or South America
- ☐ Witness a calf being born

> *I have been drunk more than once and my passion borders on madness. I regret neither.*
>
> —*Johann W. von Goethe*

- ☐ Participate in a dance-a-thon
- ☐ Put yourself on a pedestal
- ☐ Watch a professional belly dance
- ☐ Witness an Appalachian snake-handling ceremony
- ☐ Be delirious

- [ ] Have cybersex
- [ ] Write erotica
- [ ] Do a voice-over
- [ ] Go to a Gospel Mass
- [ ] Learn how other cultures give birth
- [ ] Study how other cultures bury their dead
- [ ] Build a glorious, elaborate snow castle
- [ ] Build an enormous sandman
- [ ] Sing all the verses of "Amazing Grace"
- [ ] Nurse a sick bird back to health
- [ ] See Shiprock at sunrise
- [ ] Watch *Willy Wonka and the Chocolate Factory* on a big-screen TV

- [ ] Sink a hole-in-one

- [ ] Read the Bible

- [ ] Read the Koran
  - [ ] Read between the lines

- [ ] Read the Mayan *Popol Vuh*

- [ ] Sleep on satin sheets

- [ ] Play Hamlet

- [ ] See a ghost

- [ ] Have a tea party

- [ ] Witness a revolution

- [ ] Hit a home run

- [ ] Make paper snowflakes

- [ ] Put glow-in-the-dark stars and asteroids in your room

- [ ] Catch a butterfly, then let it go

- [ ] Protest something

- [ ] Levitate someone

- [ ] Have a seance

- [ ] Learn how to say "I love you" in ten different languages

- [ ] Learn to sing "Happy Birthday" in three languages 🎂🎂🎂

- [ ] Learn how to give a great back rub

- [ ] Deejay

- [ ] Be a clown at a children's party

- [ ] Run through a fire hydrant or a sprinkler with your clothes on

- [ ] Be in a Calvin Klein or Snapple ad

- [ ] Get your name mentioned on national television

- [ ] Play stickball
- [ ] Play dress-up
- [ ] Seduce someone
- [ ] Get seduced

> *To love with all one's soul and leave the rest to fate.*
>
> —*Vladimir Nabokov*

- [ ] Indulge
- [ ] Become an expert
- [ ] Be someone's hero
- [ ] Have a mentor
- [ ] Be a mentor

- [ ] Adopt a whale
- [ ] Have high tea
- [ ] Sleep naked
- [ ] Christmas carol with candles
- [ ] Dress up and have some brandy at a piano bar, preferably while Bobby Short performs
- [ ] Hang a hammock in your living room
- [ ] Send your dog to your neighbor's house with a message attached to his collar
- [ ] Submit your manuscript
- [ ] Send a message in a bottle
- [ ] Study pebbles
- [ ] Smile at someone on the subway

- [ ] Collect seashells
- [ ] Collect scrimshaw
- [ ] Build an igloo
- [ ] Skate a perfect figure-eight
- [ ] Spin the perfect yarn
- [ ] Spin a child
- [ ] Learn to love wrinkles
- [ ] Harmonize
- [ ] Sleep on sun-dried sheets
- [ ] Take a few weeks off and read all of *Remembrance of Things Past*
- [ ] Pay off your mortgage
- [ ] Buy a car with cash
- [ ] Get quoted in a major magazine

If there are
two courses of action,
you should take
the third.

—Yiddish proverb

- [ ] Be on the cover of *Time*
- [ ] Tour the Rockies in a recreational vehicle
- [ ] Stay an extra day
- [ ] Wear a disguise
- [ ] Create something that will still be admired in the twenty-first century

> *The trouble with being in the rat race is that even if you win, you're still a rat.*
>
> —Lily Tomlin

- [ ] Donate something anonymously to a very needy cause

- ☐ Visit the house where you were born

- ☐ Spend the winter holidays in Austria or Switzerland

- ☐ Start a conversation with a stranger

- ☐ Work at a soup kitchen on Thanksgiving

- ☐ Blow bubble gum bubbles

- ☐ Blow soap bubbles in the office

- ☐ Play the harmonica at work

- ☐ Follow the precept that the best things in life are free

- ☐ Burn the bridges to the troublesome parts and people of your life

- ☐ Stop complaining

- ☐ Organize a family reunion
- ☐ Cultivate lust in your heart
- ☐ Rethink those seven deadly sins
- ☐ Adopt a highway
- ☐ Chase rainbows
- ☐ Write thank-you notes when it isn't necessary
- ☐ Become the best friend of a rich celebrity
- ☐ Figure out how to get invited to the White House
- ☐ Send a long letter to the Pope
- ☐ Carry someone else's burden
- ☐ Arrange a sabbatical for yourself

- [ ] Have all your old home movies converted to one long nostalgic video

- [ ] Color with crayons

- [ ] See how high you can swing

- [ ] Impress your friends with a one-armed push-up

- [ ] Fingerpaint

- [ ] Record something to be played or read at your funeral

- [ ] Develop a new signature

- [ ] Throw a surprise party

- [ ] Admit that you don't know

- [ ] Play in a jug band

- [ ] Start a tradition

- [ ] Wear a feather boa to work

> *There is no cure for birth and death save to enjoy the interval.*
>
> —*George Santayana*

- ☐ Predict a trend
- ☐ Wear a boa constrictor around your neck
- ☐ Learn *The Rocky Horror Picture Show* routine by heart
- ☐ Play Santa for a needy family at Christmas
- ☐ Dance the hora
- ☐ Visit a Biosphere
- ☐ Write a fan letter

- ☐ Travel Magellan's exact route around the world

- ☐ Eat a hot tamale

- ☐ Run a used-book store

- ☐ Climb the highest summits on all seven continents

- ☐ Enjoy strawberries and cream at Wimbledon

- ☐ Try out for a professional sports team

- ☐ Write a Rap song

- ☐ Have a bluejean-drive and then send truckloads down to Central America

- ☐ Throw petals at your wedding instead of rice

- ☐ Drive a Humvee through the woods

- ☐ Propose with a painting or a pet instead of a ring
- ☐ Throw a shower for a single friend
- ☐ Start a newsletter
- ☐ Attend an art opening
- ☐ Eschew the boring
- ☐ Follow your bliss
- ☐ Married or not, go on a honeymoon
- ☐ Hit the road
- ☐ Teach English as a Second Language
- ☐ Catch a snowflake on your tongue
- ☐ Walk knee-deep in maple leaves
- ☐ Tear down a wall, literal or otherwise
- ☐ Take a four-year-old to the zoo

- [ ] Say something profound on a billboard
- [ ] Go fishin'
- [ ] Invent a new word and spread it around
- [ ] Inhale
- [ ] Beat the odds
- [ ] Exact your feelings
- [ ] Sit on more laps
- [ ] Don't take the day off; take two
- [ ] Overtip the barber at some odd time of the year
- [ ] Do nothing
- [ ] Hire a caterer to deliver dinner to your home for a week

> *To seek after beauty as an end is a wild goose chase, a will-o'-the-wisp, because it is to misunderstand the very nature of beauty, which is the normal condition of a thing being as it should be.*
>
> —Ade Bethune

- ☐ Catch a falling star
- ☐ See a rodeo
- ☐ Stay on a bucking bronco
- ☐ Teach your dog to sing
- ☐ Commit
- ☐ Soak in a hot tub
- ☐ Become the president of something

- [ ] Show up
- [ ] Slow up
- [ ] Shut up
- [ ] Have a long, slow dance with a stranger
- [ ] Write your own obituary
- [ ] Pay your respects on the beaches at Normandy
- [ ] Think and grow rich
- [ ] Have someone feed you a succulent pomegranate
- [ ] Get a really good foot massage
- [ ] Cut off a bad relationship
- [ ] Chuckle

- [ ] Introduce someone to Bach, Brubeck, or the Beatles
- [ ] Change your mind
- [ ] Learn some birdcalls
- [ ] Have something public named after you
- [ ] Rally the troops
- [ ] Learn the difference between early and late
- [ ] Take up knitting
- [ ] Take your time
- [ ] Frame all your accomplishments
- [ ] Congratulate and praise lots more people
- [ ] Smell the flowers, the cooking, the rain, and the sweat

I never let
my schooling
interfere with
my education.

—Mark Twain

> *The road of excess leads to the palace of wisdom.*
>
> —William Blake

- [ ] Tell the truth, especially when it's hard
- [ ] Inscribe a book
- [ ] Have delusions of grandeur
- [ ] Be gainfully self-employed
- [ ] Lie on the couch and feed bonbons to your lover
- [ ] Be a big brother or sister to a kid
- [ ] Find the needle in the haystack
- [ ] Check in with a lover from your past

☐ Chop wood

☐ Close the bar

☐ Dance till dawn

☐ Watch the sun rise on a Hawaiian isle

☐ See the jungle when it's wet with rain

☐ Bake brownies

☐ Drink an egg cream made with Fox's U-Bet

☐ Try Hatha Yoga

☐ Read *The Relaxation Response*

☐ Stop complaining, stop explaining

☐ Learn to carve a turkey like a chef

☐ Buck the odds

☐ Fly upside down

- [ ] Rise to the occasion
- [ ] Twirl a basketball on one finger
- [ ] Get past twenty push-ups
- [ ] See how far you can swim underwater
- [ ] Push a fat boulder off a cliff
- [ ] Set your sights higher
- [ ] Hug and kiss your relatives a lot more
- [ ] Own a king-size bed
- [ ] Move
- [ ] Take a walk in the woods at night when it's snowing
- [ ] Write what you remember before you forget
- [ ] Attend the Winter Solstice, or any Paul Winter concert

- ☐ Learn to juggle more than three balls
- ☐ Pull quarters from someone's ear
- ☐ Hang up on an unwanted caller
- ☐ Spend a couple of days going to shows in London
- ☐ Baby-sit
- ☐ Plan the perfect crime and sell it to Hollywood as a screenplay
- ☐ Compete on "Jeopardy"
- ☐ Live primitively
- ☐ Shed nonessentials
- ☐ Be silent for a week
- ☐ Follow the yellow brick road
- ☐ Flaunt it

> *Our care should not be to have lived long, but to have lived long enough.*
>
> *—Seneca*

☐ Consort with cosmopolitans

☐ Be a die-hard fan

☐ Attend a Little League game

☐ Take a cross-country train ride

☐ Have yourself paged at Madison Square Garden

☐ Bet with a bookie

☐ Play croquet

☐ Play badminton

- ☐ Retire gracefully
- ☐ Write an anonymous letter
- ☐ Tend bar
- ☐ Wheedle a press pass
- ☐ Listen to all of Frank Sinatra's recordings
- ☐ Jam with the three Beatles
- ☐ Build a log cabin
- ☐ Make pancakes
- ☐ Name your body parts
- ☐ Sip Jack Daniel's
- ☐ Sing your own rendition of "Fever"
- ☐ Keep a journal
- ☐ Wine and dine someone who deserves it

> *The thing is to become a master and in your old age to acquire the courage to do what children did when they knew nothing.*
>
> —Henry Miller

- ☐ Organize a potluck supper
- ☐ Buy a perfect tomato from a farm stand and eat it like an apple
- ☐ Build the perfect fire
- ☐ Do some work for Habitat for Humanity
- ☐ Write a letter to your Congressperson
- ☐ Attend a town meeting
- ☐ Get involved

- [ ] Appear in a music video
- [ ] Bake the best apple pie
- [ ] Grow the largest pumpkin
- [ ] Raise ribbon-winning livestock
- [ ] Give a friend a copy of your favorite novel
- [ ] Start a wave at the stadium
- [ ] Be the clown in the dunking booth
- [ ] Finish school
- [ ] Be more persuasive
- [ ] Take a tour of movie stars' homes
- [ ] Ride the Circle Line around Manhattan
- [ ] Ride a cable car in San Francisco

☐ Sail a yacht down the Miami Intercoastal

☐ Board the river tour in Chicago

☐ Tear a phone book in half with your bare hands

☐ Ride a merry-go-round

☐ Have your own carnival stand

☐ Eat salt water taffy and cotton candy

☐ Sing Christmas carols around the middle of August

☐ Stop making New Year's resolutions

☐ Arrange sweet surprises

☐ Write the ending

☐ Live without a phone for a full seven days

- [ ] Overcome your most dreaded fear

- [ ] Learn to play bridge

- [ ] Admit that it's too hard and try again

- [ ] Hold out until he, she, or it gets it right

> *Insisting on perfect safety is for people who don't have the balls to live in the real world.*
>
> —Mary Schafer

- [ ] Eat, drink, and be very merry

- [ ] Bask in the glow of praise

- [ ] Give something wonderful anonymously

- [ ] Leave someone a surprise in your will

- ☐ Add a codicil to your will that tells people why you love them

- ☐ Have only one or two credit cards

- ☐ Know the best public restrooms in major cities

- ☐ Read the Bible as history and literature

- ☐ Collect large African insects

- ☐ Collect autographs

- ☐ Climb way up in a weeping willow or old copper beech tree

- ☐ Listen to whales

- ☐ Make some mean old sourpuss laugh

- ☐ Have a great bumper sticker

- ☐ Perfect your pet impersonation

- ☐ Listen to the original Jerky Boys tape

- ☐ Sit on the fifty-yard line at the Super Bowl
- ☐ Get to at least one opening day of baseball
- ☐ Realize it's not un-American to hate baseball
- ☐ Write out your wish list
- ☐ Have an epic interest in people
- ☐ Practice smiling
- ☐ Have a hideout
- ☐ Have your favorite books bound in leather
- ☐ Be known for your toasts
- ☐ Safari
- ☐ Write "If only I had . . ." on a piece of paper and flush it down the toilet

> *I went to the woods because I wished to live deliberately, to confront only the essential facts of life and see if I could not learn what it had to teach, and not, when I came to die, discover that I had not lived.*
>
> —Henry David Thoreau

- ☐ Hang a spoon from your nose
- ☐ Keep an aquarium
- ☐ Share the wealth
- ☐ Get good at black and white photography
- ☐ Come of age

☐ Get a bit part in "Friends," "Seinfeld," or "Saturday Night Live"

☐ Have your portrait painted in oils

☐ Try group therapy and don't hold back

☐ Say good-bye to your therapist

☐ Take everything off your desk and start all over

☐ Separate from your significant other for one month

☐ Buy a sarong

☐ Write a personal note on every Christmas card

☐ Have a cookout that ends with S'mores

☐ Put twenty bucks in the slots or on a nag

☐ Tell ghost stories in a pitch-black room

☐ Address the United Nations

☐ Hang a prism

☐ Feed and shelter the homeless

☐ Visit the sick

☐ Ride in a cherry picker

☐ Swing from limb to limb

☐ Go to a bed-and-breakfast one week
from today

☐ Write or paint directly
from your subconscious

☐ Turn off all the lights and slow dance
on the porch

☐ Leave love notes in large print

☐ Tango

- [ ] Plan the dreams you want to have when you're asleep

- [ ] Always be too young to take up golf

- [ ] Take up golf

- [ ] Stretch every muscle every day

- [ ] Eat your vegetables

---

> *He who hesitates is not only lost, but miles from the next exit.*
>
> —*Unknown*

---

- [ ] Unearth an amazing archaeological discovery

- [ ] Enjoy the moment without expecting it to last

☐ Appreciate gray hair

☐ Coin a phrase

☐ Don't get soft

☐ Get a Mister Softee

☐ Vote for equal rights every time

☐ Develop your own recipe for chili

☐ Listen to Bessie Smith

☐ Make your own lunch

☐ Wear a scarlet A and see what happens

☐ Proclaim a holiday

☐ Say things like "eureka," "hallelujah," and "balderdash"

☐ Prophesy prosperity

My life is passing before my eyes.
The worst part is
that I'm driving a used car.

—Woody Allen

- [ ] Dance down the staircase like Fred Astaire
- [ ] Perform one of Houdini's tricks
- [ ] Shed your inhibitions two-by-two
- [ ] Be the last to stop applauding
- [ ] Shout "Bravo" at the end of a good movie
- [ ] Develop an air of mystery
- [ ] Mend a broken heart
- [ ] Have phone sex
- [ ] Prick pretentiousness and snobbery
- [ ] Get a gold tooth, or have it capped
- [ ] Own an expensive diamond
- [ ] Write a long stream-of-consciousness note to yourself

> *What a strange machine man is!*
> *You fill him with bread, wine, fish,*
> *and radishes, and out come sighs,*
> *laughter, and dreams.*
>
> —*Nikos Kazantzakis*

- [ ] Yell like Tarzan and howl like a coyote

- [ ] Permit yourself to like a piece of art without knowing why

- [ ] Figure out how to make enough money

- [ ] Have only one PIN number

- [ ] Express absurd opinions seriously and see who listens

- [ ] Teach leadership

- [ ] Compete in a potato sack race

- ☐ Overdo a good thing
- ☐ Eat dessert first
- ☐ Attend an outdoor bluegrass festival
- ☐ Learn to play a fiddle or a uke
- ☐ Have a closet lined in cedar
- ☐ Improve your doodles
- ☐ Have a booth at a flea market
- ☐ Install a skylight over your bed
- ☐ Have a fireplace or a wood stove
- ☐ Join the polar bear club
- ☐ Till a field
- ☐ Date a supermodel
- ☐ Improve something in the world besides yourself

- ☐ Take a natural vacation at a nudist colony

- ☐ Get paid what your are worth and vice versa

- ☐ Send dozens of postcards for no particular reason

- ☐ Finish a game of Risk

- ☐ Write a long, interesting letter to faraway friends

- ☐ Grow a handlebar mustache or mutton chops

- ☐ Stop at a cathedral at night when it's empty

- ☐ Talk with your mouth full

- ☐ Get a facial

> *One of the symptoms of an approaching nervous break-down is the belief that one's work is terribly important.*
>
> —Bertrand Russell

☐ Risk saying no more often

☐ *69 someone

☐ Live in a yurt or a tepee for a while

☐ Join a volunteer fire department

☐ Climb the cone of a volcano

☐ Cut the cord and, if necessary, the apron strings

☐ Get to know your neighbors

- [ ] Have a vegetable garden
- [ ] Print your motto on your personal checks
- [ ] Watch a building being demolished or blown up

- [ ] Slide down the brass fire pole
- [ ] Reinvent the wheel
- [ ] Imagine the most pleasurable fill-in-the-blank
- [ ] Dive off a cliff into the water
- [ ] Go back to your grade school and see if you can climb the rope to the top
- [ ] Use a chain saw and a wood chipper
- [ ] Know the difference between aa and pahoehoe

Early to rise
and early to bed
makes a man healthy,
wealthy and dead.

—James Thurber

- [ ] Drink the milk from a coconut with a straw

- [ ] Love to loaf, loaf to live, and live to loaf

- [ ] Embrace chaos

- [ ] Accept ambiguity

- [ ] Have enough to retire gracefully

- [ ] Walk across a suspension bridge

- [ ] Ask to spend the night in jail

- [ ] Swim with the sharks

- [ ] Thwart a mugger

- [ ] Have five or six showerheads

- [ ] Keep meetings short and productive

- [ ] Cut your own name in stone so it will last forever

> *Everything has been figured
> except how to live.*
>
> —Jean-Paul Sartre

☐ Climb every mountain

☐ Ford every stream

☐ Be a colonel in the war on poverty

☐ Take the ferry to Ellis Island and the
Statue of Liberty

☐ Get a doctorate

☐ Take a course at or get a degree from
Harvard

☐ Get out of debt

☐ Wear silk pajamas

- [ ] Get into the highest tax bracket
- [ ] One day spend $1,000 in cash on at least six things
- [ ] Show off your fifty-yard-line tickets for the Army-Navy game
- [ ] Throw your own tailgate party
- [ ] Be nimble, spry, lithe, and elastic
- [ ] Run a personal ad
- [ ] Drop ten pounds
- [ ] Travel around the world by sailboat
- [ ] Be known as a heretic
- [ ] Think of sex as a gourmet dinner
- [ ] Pursue the one you love
- [ ] Develop a taste for Scotch, Prokofiev, or Pynchon

- ☐ Give a keynote address
- ☐ Fall asleep counting your blessings
- ☐ Execute a perfect Chevy Chase pratfall
- ☐ Be in a chase scene
- ☐ Fence
- ☐ Mambo
- ☐ Learn to use a gun, but never have to
- ☐ Get good—really good—at pool and darts
- ☐ Bowl a 300
- ☐ Wander in the Scottish heather
- ☐ Weave
- ☐ Audition for a part in *Rent* or *Annie*
- ☐ Whale-watch

- ☐ See the Loch Ness monster

- ☐ Find a masterpiece at a garage sale

- ☐ Meet your lover at the door wearing nothing but Saran Wrap

- ☐ Ride a winged horse

- ☐ Grow long hair

- ☐ Win an apology and a fat refund from the IRS

- ☐ Be a pen pal

- ☐ Bring back, and update, the Roman orgy

- ☐ Water-ski in your bare feet

- ☐ Take a child with you to cut down a Christmas tree on a snowy night

- ☐ See Stonehenge and join the Druids

☐ Hit the bell at a carnival

☐ Ride a motorcycle south
on U.S.1 in California

☐ Read Rainer Maria
Rilke

☐ Address the nation

☐ Administer the Heimlich maneuver
successfully

☐ Float

---

*A person with a hundred inter-
ests is twice as alive as one with
only fifty and four times as alive
as the man who has only twenty-
five.*

—Norman Vincent Peale

- [ ] Introduce two people who soon get married
- [ ] Profess your loves and hates
- [ ] Comfort the afflicted
- [ ] Hire someone to wrap all your Christmas presents
- [ ] Ward off an invasion
- [ ] Enjoy at least one bad habit
- [ ] Hike in the Swiss Alps
- [ ] Enter a Pro-Am tournament
- [ ] Pan for gold
- [ ] Go down into a coal mine
- [ ] Depose a witness
- [ ] Exorcize demons

- [ ] Partake in a demonstration
- [ ] Abolish the death penalty
- [ ] Make a list of all your desires
- [ ] Have an architect design the house in your head
- [ ] Reach the peak of Kilimanjaro
- [ ] Play detective
- [ ] Walk on stilts
- [ ] Pick a lock
- [ ] Kick the extra point
- [ ] Feed a baby
- [ ] Take a hansom cab ride
- [ ] Roll on a log
- [ ] See all fifty states

- [ ] Write a passionate love poem
- [ ] Make a killing on the stock market
- [ ] Learn how to use a compass
- [ ] Leave the bed unmade for a month
- [ ] Pilot a plane
- [ ] Use a seesaw
- [ ] Move an audience to tears
- [ ] Save the unicorn from extinction
- [ ] Pass mouthfuls of wine to your lover
- [ ] Ask for the best seat in the house
- [ ] Travel Route 66
- [ ] Wear pajamas all day long
- [ ] Know where you stand
- [ ] Skydive

☐ Hem your own pants

☐ Sign checks with a crayon

☐ Eat candy for breakfast

☐ Jump into a big pile of leaves

☐ Own an original Matisse, Basquiat, or Nauman

☐ Complete *The New York Times* Sunday crossword puzzle

☐ Read the entire Sunday *Times* cover to cover

☐ Tell your age proudly

☐ Wear a lampshade on your head at a black-tie event

☐ Learn all there is to know about the polka

- [ ] Pull an all-nighter
- [ ] Be the life of the party
- [ ] Join the circus

> *After all is said and done, more is said than done.*
>
> —*Unknown*

- [ ] Call a psychic hotline and discover your past lives
- [ ] Raise your own livestock
- [ ] Order a peanut butter and jelly sandwich at a business lunch
- [ ] Win a game of Trivial Pursuit

- ☐ Service your own car
- ☐ Ride in a stretch limo on a first date
- ☐ Make a gingerbread house from scratch
- ☐ Smile, relentlessly, at a grumpy person
- ☐ Have a picnic on the beach in February
- ☐ Create your own Love Potion Number 9
- ☐ Study at a culinary arts institute
- ☐ Buy someone a present for no reason at all
- ☐ Read *The Story of O* to your lover
- ☐ Dance the Macarena with Mickey Mouse
- ☐ Read the Marquis de Sade

If you stuff yourself full of poems,
essays, plays, stories, novels, films,
comic strips, magazines, music,
you automatically explode every
morning like Old Faithful.
I have never had a dry spell in my
life, mainly because I feed myself
well, to the point of bursting.
I wake early and hear my
morning voices leaping around in
my head like jumping beans.
I get out of bed to trap them
before they escape.

—Ray Bradbury

- ☐ Make the Joneses keep up with you
- ☐ Start a trend
- ☐ Be a chimney sweep for a day
- ☐ Wear stripes, florals, and plaids together
- ☐ Look after you leap
- ☐ Order from the kid's menu
- ☐ Shop at a farmer's market
- ☐ Swim the English Channel
- ☐ Swim around Manhattan
- ☐ Tap, with pride, at the Macy's Tap-A-Thon
- ☐ Play with your food
- ☐ Vamp

- [ ] Vogue
- [ ] Reread old love letters
- [ ] Rekindle a flame
- [ ] Comprehend the laws of physics

> *You are always on your way to a miracle.*
>
> —*Sark*

- [ ] Take a bubble bath built for two
- [ ] Learn to program the VCR
- [ ] Set an example
- [ ] Write poetry while sitting in a Parisian or Venetian cafe
- [ ] Become a living legend

- ☐ Own your own plot of land
- ☐ Savor moonshine
- ☐ Send all your Christmas cards out on time
- ☐ Coach Little League
- ☐ Learn Morse code
- ☐ Eat only the green M&M's
- ☐ Travel the B&O Railroad
- ☐ Eat humble pie
- ☐ Take pride in your offspring
- ☐ Learn and practice moxie
- ☐ Discover the roots of your first name
- ☐ Become familiar with ferns
- ☐ Do away with your Achilles' heel

- ☐ Act up
- ☐ Act your shoe size
- ☐ Serve on a jury
- ☐ Hire a valet
- ☐ Ask for a discount
- ☐ Astonish and amaze yourself
- ☐ Write a love note in lipstick or shaving cream on the bathroom mirror
- ☐ Read at a bar mitzvah
- ☐ Bear witness
- ☐ Pretend you're French
- ☐ Call Larry King's show
- ☐ Live in a trailer
- ☐ Sign autographs

- [ ] Annoy Imus and Howard Stern

- [ ] Skip the gym and go shopping

- [ ] Become familiar with the facade of Notre Dame de Paris

- [ ] Contemplate beauty at the Sainte-Chapelle in Paris

- [ ] Pay your respects

- [ ] Mourn the dead at Auschwitz

> *We don't know a millionth of one percent about anything.*
>
> —*Thomas A. Edison*

- [ ] Change someone's mind

- [ ] Enjoy your mother-in-law's company

- [ ] Relisten to the first cassette you ever bought
- [ ] Write to your lover in code
- [ ] Create a challenge course in your backyard
- [ ] Hang a tire swing from a tree
- [ ] Quote a rapper
- [ ] Go to a nightclub in drag
- [ ] Use handcuffs
- [ ] Do it in the road
- [ ] Have passion for your work
- [ ] Leave a fifty in a blind person's cup
- [ ] Revel in raw sex
- [ ] Let the phone ring

- ☐ Administer last rites
- ☐ Practice sitting up straight
- ☐ Wear a kilt to a formal affair
- ☐ Fall in love on a first date
- ☐ Convince your mom to get a mammogram
- ☐ Start a pillow fight
- ☐ Invite your friends over for a slumber party
- ☐ Realize it's okay to not want a baby
- ☐ Make the perfect Bloody Mary
- ☐ Learn to ride western like the Marlboro Man
- ☐ Impress the sommelier
- ☐ Send him a dozen red roses

- [ ] Be a godparent
- [ ] Wow your friends with your karaoke routine
- [ ] Track down someone who influenced you
- [ ] Tend the keg at a fraternity bash
- [ ] Start a nude room at a party
- [ ] Cast a spell
- [ ] Buy an entire Western ensemble from Billy Martin's

- [ ] Change your last name
- [ ] Get your picture taken in a champagne tub in the Poconos
- [ ] Wear a wig
- [ ] Be a guest on "Letterman"

- [ ] Buy a complete set of Dickens or Sherlock Holmes

- [ ] Operate your own bed & breakfast

- [ ] Memorize all the presidents of the United States

- [ ] Thank a veteran

- [ ] Attend a peace rally

- [ ] Sleep with your dog

- [ ] Save a tree

- [ ] Maintain an absolutely perfect credit rating

- [ ] Play hooky

- [ ] Decorate outdoors with abandon at Christmastime

- [ ] Enjoy the view from your roof

- [ ] Whoop it up

> *Please watch out for each other and love and forgive.*
>
> —Jim Henson

☐ Make no apologies for loving ABBA and the Monkees

☐ Try your hand at tatting

☐ Become a member of Mensa

☐ Collect weather vanes, Arm & Hammer Baking Soda boxes, first editions, or masks

☐ Use words like "soupçon," "frisson," and "cachet" more often

☐ Indulge your soft spot for doughnuts

☐ Lust after someone dangerous

At first people refuse to believe
that a strange new thing
can be done, and then they begin to hope
it can be done, then they see
it can be done—then it is done
and all the world wonders why
it was not done centuries ago.

—Frances Hodgson Burnett

☐ Make a fuss over your mom's cooking

☐ Lollygag

☐ Have a love affair with a movie star

☐ Organize your friends and have an
adult prom

☐ Play footsie with your date in a swank
restaurant

☐ Sweep someone off their feet

☐ Be swept off your feet

☐ Lose your cool

☐ Rejoice—the end is pretty far away

☐ Wet your pants laughing

☐ Wear rose-colored glasses or contacts

☐ Quote Frank Sinatra

> *Never, never, never under any circumstances... face facts!*
>
> **—Ruth Gordon**

☐ Tell your boss you need workman's comp for ergophobia

☐ Take a first-class ego trip

☐ Give the bus driver a present

☐ Spring clean in October

☐ Give your best friend a nickname only you can use

☐ Pack a thermos full of hot cocoa and go for a long walk in the wintry woods

☐ Repeat the phrase "Don't die wondering"

- ☐ Get a second Bachelor's degree

- ☐ Donate big bucks to your alma mater

- ☐ Choose a bridesmaid's dress everyone loves

- ☐ Register at a bookshop, gourmet food store, or L.L. Bean for your birthday

- ☐ Comb the sand for beach glass and driftwood

- ☐ Skip rocks

- ☐ Do a mitzvah

- ☐ Pretend you don't speak English

- ☐ Wear sunglasses at night

- ☐ Learn to spell hors d'oeuvres

- ☐ Commission a portrait of your dog

- [ ] Watch a session of Congress from the visitor's gallery
- [ ] Grow antique roses on a white trellis
- [ ] Make out like a bandit
- [ ] Make out like teenagers
- [ ] Attend the seventh game of the World Series
- [ ] Listen to a recording of Leontyne Price, in her prime, sing "Vissi d'arte"
- [ ] Study Latin and classical Greek
- [ ] Purchase custom-made handsewn shoes
- [ ] Bring home the bacon and fry it up in a pan
- [ ] Make love in the back of a limo
- [ ] Eat pufferfish sushi

- [ ] Place your hands in Marilyn Monroe's handprints at Mann's Chinese Theater

- [ ] Build and launch a model rocket

- [ ] Perform with your band at Jim Morrison's grave

- [ ] Take silly pictures with your best friend in a photo booth

- [ ] Wear two different shoes

- [ ] Become conversant with Symbolism, Dadaism, *Der Blau Reiter*, and Renaissance art

- [ ] Attend a couture show in Paris

- [ ] Dip into your capital

- [ ] Wax your eyebrows

- [ ] Find out if blondes do have more fun

- ☐ Be able to distinguish between acid-house, trip-hop, and native tongue
- ☐ Indulge in a two-hour body massage
- ☐ Discover where shooting stars go
- ☐ Achieve greater family happiness
- ☐ Channel your endorphins
- ☐ Engage in Homeric laughter
- ☐ Deliver a home-cooked meal to a sick friend
- ☐ Have a tummy tuck
- ☐ Have big, luscious breasts
- ☐ Be nominated for an Oscar, Tony or Emmy
- ☐ Compete in a Worst Prom Story contest—and win

- ☐ Make the most of a bald spot

- ☐ Play donkey basketball

- ☐ Attend the U.N. Conference on Women

- ☐ Discover a vaccine for something

> *"I don't see why you say a web is a miracle—it's just a web."*
>
> *"Ever try to spin one?"*
>
> —E. B. White

- ☐ Clock in at 25 mph in the 100-meter dash

- ☐ Go to Capri and don't come back

- ☐ Be a veejay

- [ ] House-sit in a penthouse

- [ ] Chimpanzee-sit for Michael Jackson

- [ ] Paint with a big brush

- [ ] Get comped at the casino

- [ ] Subscribe to every magazine you ever wanted

- [ ] Own a shoe collection to rival Imelda Marcos

- [ ] Read the fine print

- [ ] Close the biggest deal you'll ever make

- [ ] Face everyone else in the elevator

- [ ] Throw open the windows and scream "I'm mad as hell and I'm not gonna take it anymore!"

- [ ] Wear a lei

Eschew the monumental.
Shun the epic.
All the guys who can paint great big
pictures
can paint great small ones.

—Ernest Hemingway

> *Find expression for a joy and you will intensify its ecstasy.*
>
> —Oscar Wilde

- [ ] Ride the Orient Express
- [ ] Learn some dirty jokes that would make a nun laugh
- [ ] Live in Wyoming or Montana
- [ ] See the Black Hills
- [ ] Get blood from a stone and a silk purse from a sow's ear
- [ ] Own a ferret
- [ ] Own a John Philip Sousa CD

- [ ] Act out the seventy-six trombone scenes from *The Music Man*

- [ ] Carve a smiling jack-o'-lantern

- [ ] Wear a Green Bay Packer cheesehead or a green foam Statue of Liberty crown

- [ ] Purchase at least one outlandish tie

- [ ] Warm the heart with music from a harp or lute

- [ ] Get someone to teach you how to play the bagpipes

- [ ] Build close ties to your grandchildren

- [ ] Love a teddy bear

- [ ] Tell your children all about your life

- [ ] Have another cookie

- [ ] Impersonate Elvis, Jerry Lewis, Ethel Merman, or Maurice Chevalier

- [ ] Wonder

- [ ] Rage, rage against the dying of the light

- [ ] Mix the perfect cocktail

- [ ] Ask for the biggest, fattest Swiss Army knife

- [ ] Go down in a submarine

- [ ] Play in Madison Square Garden

- [ ] Forecast the future

- [ ] Wear the pants

- [ ] Press the mute

- [ ] Hire a stylist

- [ ] See and report a UFO

☐ Own a bar; drink for free

☐ Get your start at the Bitter End

☐ Claim you were at Woodstock

☐ Claim you were a Deadhead

☐ Pose for a full-page ad

☐ Be in the headlines

☐ Star in the show

☐ Direct a movie

☐ Take a mountain bike to the Ozarks

☐ Moonlight with your hobby

☐ Sell something by direct mail

☐ Jam at the Village Vanguard

☐ Throw strikes

☐ Play in the majors

- ☐ Pitch a no-hitter
- ☐ Play "The Star Spangled Banner" like Hendrix did
- ☐ Lose with true dignity
- ☐ Relearn "walk the doggie" with your yo-yo
- ☐ Send unsigned valentines to people in the office
- ☐ Outfox the bean counters
- ☐ Leave the place in better shape than you found it
- ☐ Leave the bed unmade, the toilet seat up, and the toothpaste cap off—just once
- ☐ Plant an indoor herb garden
- ☐ Embellish the good old stories

- [ ] Get your Rolodex in perfect shape

- [ ] Write out your plan for life

- [ ] Float in the Dead Sea

- [ ] Spend the night in a pyramid

- [ ] Dye your eyebrows

- [ ] Learn double dutch

> *The biggest sin is sitting on your ass.*
>
> *—Florynce Kennedy*

- [ ] Examine your tear under a microscope

- [ ] Examine a Whopper under a micro-scope

YOU NEED ONLY CLAIM
THE EVENTS OF YOUR
LIFE TO MAKE YOURSELF
YOURS. WHEN YOU TRULY
POSSESS ALL YOU HAVE
BEEN AND DONE, WHICH
MAY TAKE SOME TIME,
YOU ARE FIERCE WITH
REALITY.

—FLORIDA SCOTT MAXWELL

- [ ] Teach yourself how to repair an engine
- [ ] Buy nothing for a weekend—not even public transportation
- [ ] Propose
- [ ] Rewrite the Book of Genesis to your liking
- [ ] Wallpaper your bathroom walls with old photographs
- [ ] Pretend that everyone knows God's a woman
- [ ] Cornrow your Westie
- [ ] Recognize your own addictions
- [ ] Learn braille
- [ ] Blend your herbal teas
- [ ] Sit in an empty church

- [ ] Bake Shrinky Dinks
- [ ] Design and paint stained-glass ornaments
- [ ] Become a *Little Rascals* expert

> *It opens the lungs, washes the countenance, exercises the eyes, and softens down the temper. So cry away.*
>
> —*Charles Dickens*

- [ ] Cry copiously
- [ ] Scuba-dive for jewelry in a public lake

- [ ] Take your frustrations out at a driving range
- [ ] Have lunch with Jenny Craig
- [ ] Impersonate John Travolta
- [ ] Have your own radio show
- [ ] Examine whether or not you are a racist
- [ ] Pay a stranger's subway fare
- [ ] Watch an autopsy
- [ ] Walk a marathon with a disabled entrant
- [ ] Convince your partner to go back to school
- [ ] Enlighten racists, anti-Semites, and homophobes

☐ Have a V-8

☐ Have a Yoo-Hoo

☐ Umpire a professional ball game

☐ Ace your opponent

☐ Shoot craps

☐ Call heads *and* tails

☐ Put your affairs in order

☐ Dissolve into chaos

☐ Revel in foofaraw

☐ Use "higgledy-piggledy" in everyday conversation

☐ Approach the millennium with unchecked enthusiasm

☐ Hang ten

- [ ] Learn at least three palindromes

- [ ] Spot oxymorons

- [ ] Track a whitetail deer through the woods

- [ ] See a bighorn sheep at Estes Park in Colorado

- [ ] Camp out in the snow

- [ ] Hold up an attention-getting sign outside the "Today Show" window

- [ ] Be old enough to get a birthday greeting from the President and Willard Scott

- [ ] Get Bryant Gumble or Katie Couric to autograph this book

- [ ] Hop on board a train to who knows where

- ☐ Cop a plea
- ☐ Top someone's best line
- ☐ Have an out-of-body experience

> *It is wonderful to be young, but it is equally desirable to be mature and rich in experience.*
>
> —Bernard Baruch

- ☐ Be hypnotized
- ☐ Let someone else win
- ☐ Hit a home run over the Green Monster in Fenway Park
- ☐ Get backstage
- ☐ Shear a sheep

- ☐ Spend the day with a fireman
- ☐ Spend the day observing an emergency room
- ☐ Spend the day with a cop on his beat
- ☐ Outfox Letterman
- ☐ Be an openly gay character on prime-time TV
- ☐ Scale a fish
- ☐ Master singing scales
- ☐ Memorize people's scents
- ☐ Allow yourself to be awestruck
- ☐ Blast the *third* movement of Beethoven's Ninth Symphony
- ☐ Understate the obvious
- ☐ Emphasize the subtle

- ☐ Play hopscotch with kids
- ☐ Buy a subscription to a flower-of-the-month club
- ☐ Buy a subscription to a wine-of-the-month club
- ☐ Send steaks and lobsters to someone
- ☐ Send lox to someone
- ☐ Send a Katz's sausage to your children
- ☐ Cartwheel in the grass barefoot
- ☐ Transcend
- ☐ Absorb
- ☐ Wear your seatbelt
- ☐ Take the Meyer Briggs test and learn your psychological profile
- ☐ Share your umbrella with a stranger

- [ ] Tell the chef the pizza was perfect
- [ ] Learn to read music
- [ ] Drive a cab
- [ ] Volunteer at a hotline
- [ ] Spot people in clouds
- [ ] Build something entirely by yourself
- [ ] Perfect your Chaplin routine
- [ ] Read Rita Dove, W.H. Auden, Walt Whitman, and Leslie Marmon Silko
- [ ] Wrestle an alligator
- [ ] Start a sing-a-long, preferably "Twist and Shout," in an elevator
- [ ] Detox
- [ ] Study voodoo or Santeria

- [ ] Phone in to a radio talk show
- [ ] Take a flying lesson
- [ ] Take a flying leap
- [ ] Hire a personal shopper
- [ ] Wear stilettos
- [ ] Read, and live, the Kama Sutra
- [ ] Wear lipstick to bed (both of you)
- [ ] Hula-Hoop
- [ ] Break a tradition
- [ ] Pop a wheelie
- [ ] Picket something
- [ ] Buy the house a beer
- [ ] Buy everyone in the diner a cup of coffee

> *And whatsoever you do, do it heartily.*
>
> —*Colossians 3:23*

- ☐ Mesmerize

- ☐ Teach an old dog new tricks

- ☐ Drink the healing waters on Margaret's Island in Budapest

- ☐ Give the delivery man some coffee

- ☐ Get on the cover of a Wheaties box

- ☐ Charm

- ☐ Leave work early and take your family to dinner and a movie

- ☐ Train to be a flight attendant

- [ ] Read transgressive fiction

- [ ] Inhale helium before saying "I do"

- [ ] Eat one Raisinet at a time

- [ ] Videotape yourself eating and then play it backward

- [ ] Boogie on down

- [ ] Plant a whoopie cushion in the boardroom

- [ ] Be on "Star Search"

- [ ] Fill your bed with rose petals

- [ ] Leave loads of munchies for the baby-sitter

- [ ] Listen to the sound of love

- [ ] Feel purple

- [ ] Taste green

Man's main task in life
is to give birth to himself.

—Erich Fromm

- ☐ Reenact the love scene on the beach in *From Here to Eternity*

- ☐ Splurge on the wedding dress of your dreams

- ☐ Slip something past the censors

- ☐ Trust in yourself—not Wayne Dyer or Marianne Williamson

- ☐ Catch Wayne Newton's act in Vegas

- ☐ Stand the test of time

- ☐ Be Liz Taylor's next

- ☐ Serve as a ball person at the U.S. Open

- ☐ Get to the center of a Tootsie Roll Pop without biting

- ☐ Eat the peanut butter first in a Reeses

- ☐ Pay your dues assiduously

- [ ] Study the Talmud
- [ ] Interview a celebrity
- [ ] Rescue a kitten from a burning building
- [ ] Get a precise and expensive haircut

> *It is the nature of a man as he grows older to protest against change, particularly change for the better.*
>
> **—John Steinbeck**

- [ ] Take a mineral bath at Saratoga Springs
- [ ] Paint your toenails
- [ ] Spit off the Eiffel Tower

- ☐ Solve the mind-body problem
- ☐ Allow yourself to feel patriotic
- ☐ Be known as a citizen of the world
- ☐ Compete in a soap-box derby
- ☐ Make your own pizza
- ☐ Make a thermos full of margaritas and watch the fireworks
- ☐ Eat the mescal worm
- ☐ Donate blood
- ☐ Watch a meteor shower
- ☐ Read *A Christmas Carol*
- ☐ Be on "The Real World XXX"
- ☐ Spend New Year's Eve in Times Square

☐ Make a snow angel

☐ Make a snowman

☐ Build a snow fort

☐ Go off a rope swing into a lake

☐ Whistle back at construction workers

☐ Consider the lilies

☐ Eat a one-pound box of Godiva in one sitting without a smidgen of guilt

☐ Daydream for a whole day

☐ Shuffle like a croupier

☐ Arrange a big gabfest

☐ Tell fortunes

☐ Futz

☐ Operate heavy machinery

> *Life is either a daring adventure, or nothing. Security is mostly a superstition. It does not exist in nature, nor do the children of men as a whole experience it.*
>
> —Helen Keller

- ☐ Toast marshmallows
- ☐ Wear suspenders, garters, and a bow tie
- ☐ Have pickled herring with farmer's bread
- ☐ Be entertained by a geisha
- ☐ Gavel them into silence
- ☐ Genuflect and bow your head

- [ ] Have a private audience with the Pope or the queen

- [ ] Tip your hat to all the women in town

- [ ] Embrace your gestalt

- [ ] Sleep with a ghost in the room

- [ ] Get around, get off, get away, get ahead, and get together

- [ ] Giddap

- [ ] Fly in a helicopter to the top of a mountain and hike back down

- [ ] Make hay while the sun shines

- [ ] Watch an egg hatch

- [ ] Fall head-over-heels in love

- [ ] Take part in heaven on earth

- [ ] Take a bus or train up into the Andes

It's a delightful thing to think of perfection;
but it's vastly more amusing
to talk of errors and absurdities.

—Fanny Burney

- [ ] Drink champagne with a crazy straw
- [ ] Visit the Galapagos
- [ ] Take the helm for awhile
- [ ] Take dance lessons at Arthur Murray
- [ ] Take leave of your senses
- [ ] Blow the foghorn
- [ ] Spend a night in a lighthouse
- [ ] Be more careful, especially around ladders
- [ ] Have a personal trainer
- [ ] Look cool in a six-foot stocking cap
- [ ] Open all the windows
- [ ] Ply her with bonbons, poetry, and flowers

- ☐ Honor a local hero
- ☐ Get engaged at least once
- ☐ Ask him to marry you
- ☐ Take the SATs some years after college
- ☐ Sell Girl Scout cookies
- ☐ Study t'ai chi
- ☐ Construct a crossword puzzle and submit it to a newspaper
- ☐ Damn the torpedoes
- ☐ Deactivate a live bomb
- ☐ Spend the inheritance
- ☐ Have a ball and make it a masked one

☐ Select a wild creature for your personal totem

☐ Ignore minor infractions

☐ Join a cattle drive

☐ Rewrite it

> *"But how do you learn?"*
>
> *"The way a tennis player learns to play tennis, by making a fool of yourself, by falling on your face, by rushing the net and missing the ball, and finally by practice."*
>
> **—May Sarton**

☐ Ride shotgun in an armored van

☐ Attend the rehearsal for Judgment Day

- [ ] Count up your rites of passage
- [ ] Find the perfect recipe for risotto
- [ ] Organize an office sports tournament
- [ ] Flyfish the Battenkill in Vermont
- [ ] Cruise the backwoods of Vermont between October 7 and October 14
- [ ] Shatter the glass ceiling
- [ ] Imitate Groucho
- [ ] Stand on your very own soapbox
- [ ] Reread books from your childhood
- [ ] Be able to tie a granny, a bowline, a clove hitch, and a sheepshank
- [ ] Breathe deeply
- [ ] Start a rumor and see how fast it comes around

- [ ] Kiss people on both cheeks

- [ ] Watch the salmon run

- [ ] Salivate over something before digging in

- [ ] Try the Arch Deluxe

- [ ] Create an annual family ritual of some kind

- [ ] Save up

- [ ] See a three-dimensional image on a scanning microscope

- [ ] Amaze

- [ ] Wear scanties

- [ ] Take it one day at a time

- [ ] Decide on a favorite color and a lucky number

- ☐ Spend a day at the track
- ☐ Brainstorm
- ☐ Laugh out loud
- ☐ Say something nice to the tolltaker
- ☐ Keep the sabbath
- ☐ Have a day of rest
- ☐ Wade in hip boots
- ☐ Perfect your Pig Latin
- ☐ Leave cookies and milk for Santa Claus
- ☐ Make a memory jar
- ☐ Research the subject you've always wanted to know about
- ☐ Marry a royal

> *I know of only one duty, and that is to love.*
>
> —*Albert Camus*

- [ ] Snowshoe
- [ ] Suction-cup a birdfeeder on to the window
- [ ] Try exotic spices
- [ ] Lose yourself in the masses
- [ ] Fill a type tray with bits and pieces of your life
- [ ] See if acupuncture works for you
- [ ] Cure something
- [ ] Mud-wrestle

☐ Pause inside a covered bridge

☐ Share a pound of caviar

☐ Steal the show

☐ Let your hair down and the chips fall

☐ Play Spud

☐ Apply to go up in the Goodyear Blimp

☐ Make a reservation for a trip to the moon

☐ Read banned books

☐ Lay bricks

☐ Crew in a sailboat race

☐ Be clairvoyant

☐ Play with clay

☐ Recycle vigorously

- ☐ Take part in a raindance
- ☐ Compost
- ☐ Control the cost
- ☐ Watch beavers build a dam
- ☐ Ride in a dumbwaiter before they are extinct
- ☐ See a full eclipse
- ☐ Duck out of the rat race
- ☐ Appreciate love handles
- ☐ Study the lessons of history
- ☐ Contemplate your navel
- ☐ Touch your elbows behind your back
- ☐ Touch your tongue to your nose
- ☐ Be an informed source

> *There is no heavier burden than a great potential.*
>
> —*Charlie Brown*

- [ ] Rent a jukebox
- [ ] Show up for jury duty
- [ ] Make fun of the Ku Klux Klan
- [ ] Get yourself a vanity license plate
- [ ] Take a lie detector test
- [ ] Change your lifestyle
- [ ] Eat real key lime pie
- [ ] Practice reading lips
- [ ] Lend money with no questions asked

☐ Watch your favorite childhood movie
with your son or daughter

☐ Don't knock it till you've tried it

☐ Massage someone's ego

☐ Learn first aid

☐ Have a method to your madness

☐ Moped in Bermuda

☐ Snorkel in St. John

☐ Come home for a nooner

☐ Go deep

☐ Navigate the shoals

☐ Crew on a sloop

☐ Assess your needs

☐ Accept mortality, but live forever

☐ Meet your lover at a motel

- ☐ Negotiate a better deal
- ☐ Network
- ☐ Clip coupons
- ☐ Nurse someone back to health
- ☐ Join the Peace Corps
- ☐ Hire a private detective
- ☐ Share the profits
- ☐ Needlepoint your favorite proverb
- ☐ Pump iron
- ☐ Rethink first impressions
- ☐ Set up a scholarship
- ☐ Shingle a roof
- ☐ Read the fine print
- ☐ Supplement your income

The need for change
bulldozed a road down
the center of my mind.

—Maya Angelou

☐ Barter your skills

☐ Find a buried treasure

☐ Spot one of America's Most Wanted

☐ Win on "America's Funniest Home Videos"

☐ Grow wildflowers 🌼🌼🌼🌼🌼

☐ Clean up the mess

☐ Give up being perfect

☐ Understand the sound of one hand clapping

☐ Restore your grandparents' wedding photo

☐ Bathe in the lap of luxury

☐ Be childlike, not childish

☐ Lay it on the line for the sake of principle

- [ ] Read bedtime stories

- [ ] Read the Beatitudes

- [ ] Win an amateur photography competition

- [ ] *Caveat emptor*

- [ ] Blow off the obsequious

- [ ] Jump out of the cake

> *Every survival kit should include a sense of humor.*
>
> —*Anonymous*

- [ ] Know the way out and way in

- [ ] Consider the opposite

- [ ] Orbit the earth

Civilization has taught us
to eat with a fork,
but even now,
if nobody is around,
we use our fingers.

—Will Rogers

- [ ] Go undercover with a tape recorder

- [ ] Wear a virtual reality helmet

- [ ] Allow yourself an outburst

- [ ] Sing in a glee club, a capella group, or barbershop quartet

- [ ] Come from behind

- [ ] Defy gravity

- [ ] Pledge money to public television or radio

- [ ] Master a kinky technique

- [ ] Meet the love of your life's ex, and shake his or her hand and say "thank you"

- [ ] Chase a tornado

- [ ] Memorize "Jabberwocky"

- [ ] Buy a sex toy

- [ ] Experience Brazilian Carnaval

- [ ] Fall in love on public transportation

- [ ] Read Kerouac, Ginsberg, Corso, and Burroughs

- [ ] Play bebop

---

*Work is love made visible.*

—*Kahlil Gibran*

---

- [ ] Live in a Soho loft

- [ ] Coin a great label for a generation

- [ ] Make homemade tortillas

- [ ] Tell everyone special to you that you love them

☐ Attend the tulip festival in Seattle

☐ Spend a few days in a place where you are the minority

☐ Understand what loneliness really means

☐ Make everything in your life a crescendo

☐ Be a superhero

☐ Get to the Final Frontier on the Star Trek pinball game

☐ Have Don Ho play the ukelele at your very own luau

☐ Go up the down escalator

☐ Buy the best seat in the house for a play with great reviews

☐ Roll down a small hill

- [ ] Go sleighriding
- [ ] Rotate the tires, or the Rollerblade wheels
- [ ] Hustle
- [ ] Master grilling techniques
- [ ] Quarrel calmly
- [ ] Drop names
- [ ] Ask for a raise
- [ ] Give raises
- [ ] Saunter, slither, or sashay
- [ ] Use a two-person saw
- [ ] Scavenge dumpsters for their treasures
- [ ] R.S.V.P.
- [ ] Be known for your baking

☐ Sell out if the price is right and you're happy

☐ Be serious

☐ Keep a stiff upper lip

☐ Let your hair down

☐ Keep your ear to the ground

☐ Stick your neck out

☐ Save your leftovers and give them to the hungry

☐ Have press credentials

☐ Sin no more

☐ Appear on a soap opera

☐ Soap up your partner

☐ Offer solace

> *Let us strive to Awaken,*
> *Awaken. Take heed, do not squander your life.*
>
> *—An evening prayer*
> *(Zen Buddhism)*

- ☐ Soothe a wounded ego
- ☐ Sponsor a team, a race car, or a fundraising event
- ☐ Invest in a Broadway show
- ☐ Stand in as a double
- ☐ Be a stuntperson and learn to fall off buildings
- ☐ Charge $300 an hour for your advice
- ☐ Scoop a major publication

☐ **Streak the Junior League**

☐ **Resuscitate someone**

☐ **Exercise eight days a week**

☐ **Stroll the Champs-Elysées**

☐ **Have five minutes in the Oval Office**

☐ **Win a spelling bee**

☐ **Do lunch with _____**

☐ **Pack the suggestion box with your ideas**

☐ **Surround yourself with trust**

☐ **Sit on the Supreme Court**

☐ **Buy a pair of leather pants**

☐ **See the good in those with whom you differ**

☐ Hear a newborn baby cry

☐ Listen to a sermon given by the Pope

☐ Mingle

☐ Know ecstasy

☐ Remember the seeds beneath the snow

☐ Bring up a moral child

☐ Create a story quilt

☐ Immerse yourself in another culture

☐ Stop daydreaming and seek your fortune

☐ Vary the seating

☐ Read all the stuff that comes home from school

☐ Encourage enterprise

- [ ] Reach out and touch someone
- [ ] Start with the air you breathe and list all the good things in your life
- [ ] Relive those thrilling days of yesteryear
- [ ] Get eight hours of sleep every night
- [ ] Lead, follow, or get out of the way
- [ ] Live without a cellular phone
- [ ] Drive a pickup that is at least fifteen years old
- [ ] Apprentice yourself to a cabinetmaker
- [ ] Be Woody Allen's therapist
- [ ] Send cartons of goodies to kids at camp

- [ ] Make a clambake happen
- [ ] Charm a snake
- [ ] See the Taj Mahal
- [ ] Perform a riff with Wynton Marsalis
- [ ] Stop a mall from being built
- [ ] Raise emus
- [ ] Have a private master class with Baryshnikov
- [ ] Barrel down Niagara Falls
- [ ] Serve prosciutto with melon at your next affair
- [ ] Dance in Red Square at midnight
- [ ] Surprise someone with Swedish fish
- [ ] Benchpress your weight

> *For love is not like a river, confined between two banks. Its very essence is to overflow.*
>
> —*Mike Mason*

☐ Put flowers on the untended grave of a stranger

☐ Join the Wrigley Field Bleacher Bums for one day and root for the Cubs

☐ Dress up and go trick or treating

☐ Locate and call a childhood friend you haven't communicated with in at least twenty years

☐ Learn who Snoop-Doggy Dogg, Beck, Sapphire, and Sparrow are

☐ Try being a vegan

- [ ] Be caricatured in a Barnes & Noble ad

- [ ] Own a kooky umbrella

- [ ] View the complete works of Fellini—in Italy

- [ ] Write all that you remember of your family history for the next generations

- [ ] Have your own talk show

- [ ] Ride a swan boat in Boston Commons

> *The young do not know enough to be prudent, and therefore, they attempt the impossible—and achieve it, generation after generation.*
>
> —Pearl S. Buck

☐ Invite all of the childhood friends you can find to a reunion at your residence

☐ Send a friend flowers for no particular reason on no special day

☐ Go to a professional football game and cheer for everyone on both teams

☐ Play ghost in the graveyard on a summer night

☐ Write a letter to the editor of your local newspaper praising someone in public life

☐ Set up an annual award honoring your favorite teacher

☐ Find your favorite childhood book and read it to a child

☐ Take an incapacitated neighbor to vote

- [ ] Participate in a Neighbor-hood Watch Program

- [ ] Search for the bullion of the Huachuca Canyon gold

- [ ] Spend at least two hours of quality time a day with your dog

- [ ] Identify a tree's age by counting the rings on its trunk

- [ ] Splurge on courtside, season tickets to the Lakers

- [ ] Detect a forgery

- [ ] Sit for Hirschfeld and find the Ninas in your portrait

- [ ] Volley with Martina Navratilova

- [ ] Sing along with Andy Williams to "Moon River"

> "Let God do it all," someone
> will say; but if man folds his
> arms, God will go to sleep.
>
> —Miguel de Unamuno y Jugo

☐ Break the tape at a triathlon

☐ Debut at the Grand Ole Opry or
the Apollo

☐ Get published in *Harper's*

☐ Root for the return of the Horn and
Hardhardt Automat

☐ Become an Avon Lady—or Gentleman

☐ Sing at a wedding

☐ Go back and spend the night at your
old sleepaway camp

- [ ] Become so good at white water rafting that you can be a guide on the most difficult rivers
- [ ] Skate the lead in the Ice Capades
- [ ] Be a write-in on the ballot
- [ ] Design a musical instrument
- [ ] Sponsor a needy child
- [ ] Travel the world with J. Peterman
- [ ] Celebrate your hairdresser at the Barbering Hall of Fame
- [ ] Start your own cosmetics line
- [ ] Learn to recognize iambic pentameter
- [ ] Overcome adversity
- [ ] Survive
- [ ] Comfort the afflicted

EVERYTHING HAS BEEN
THOUGHT OF BEFORE,
BUT THE PROBLEM IS
TO THINK OF IT AGAIN.

—JOHANN W. VON GOETHE

- [ ] Make a weekly visit to your local library
- [ ] Compete in the Elephant Polo Tournament in Nepal
- [ ] Skitch
- [ ] Turn out the lights and watch *Wait Until Dark*
- [ ] Be a Beatnik, Hippie, Punk, or Rude Boy
- [ ] Tell your children you were a Beatnik, Hippie, Punk, or Rude Boy
- [ ] Gather up your friends for a quilting bee
- [ ] Learn to throw your voice
- [ ] Climb the slippery slope
- [ ] Have bangers and mash

> *Life shrinks or expands in proportion to one's courage.*
>
> —Anaïs Nin

- [ ] Compose a fairy tale

- [ ] Act out a fairy tale

- [ ] Be ringmaster for a day at Ringling Brothers

- [ ] Be the person who pulls or announces the Lotto numbers on TV

- [ ] Bounce at the Viper Lounge

- [ ] Dust off them blue suede shoes

- [ ] Ably describe honky-tonk, ska, and high-lonesome

- ☐ Weave your way through the loopholes
- ☐ Get a full-body tan
- ☐ Have your monograph published
- ☐ Make the first string
- ☐ Make Donny Osmond serenade you with "Puppy Love"
- ☐ Devise your own definition of beauty
- ☐ Spend a day watching the entire *Rocky*, *Star Wars*, or *Friday XIII* collection on video
- ☐ Portage a canoe
- ☐ Have your own website
- ☐ Read a big, thick Russian novel
- ☐ Apprehend a drug lord

☐ Amaze your friends by memorizing all the U.S. vice presidents

☐ Become fluent in cyberspeak

☐ Attend a foam rave

☐ Gather a bunch of friends for a Halloween hayride

☐ Jet-ski in choppy waters

☐ Raise ants, bees, or worms

☐ Frame all your past and present business cards

☐ Hang mistletoe in August

☐ Be able to explain a hedge fund, risk arbitrage, and a mutual fund

☐ Learn to communicate with animals

☐ Hang out with a revolutionary

> *To die for the revolution is a one-shot deal; to live for the revolution means taking on the more difficult commitment of changing our day-to-day life patterns.*
>
> —**Will Rogers**

- [ ] Rappel

- [ ] Be there when the drill hits a gusher

- [ ] Learn to love words like Nabokov

- [ ] Live within your means

- [ ] Beat an incurable disease

- [ ] Interview J. D. Salinger and ask him to tell you about his father, the butter and egg man

- [ ] Release balloons in church
- [ ] Put a scavenger hunt in your will
- [ ] Quote Derrida, Foucault, or Berra
- [ ] Cross the international dateline and get to yesterday
- [ ] Have an advice column
- [ ] Befriend a shaman, mystic, or priestess
- [ ] Show intimations of immortality
- [ ] Improve your intuition
- [ ] Scat like a pro
- [ ] Hit the jackpot
- [ ] Be a painter's model
- [ ] Play in the Orpheus Chamber Orchestra
- [ ] Swoon over a star

- ☐ Appreciate the larceny in your heart
- ☐ Leak a really hot story
- ☐ Ride a camel to the Pyramids
- ☐ Stake a claim
- ☐ Astound the doubters
- ☐ Outfox the dealers at an auction
- ☐ Cook dinner in the fireplace
- ☐ Get your name in a gossip column
- ☐ See Michelangelo's David
- ☐ Meet John F. Kennedy, Jr.
- ☐ Shake hands with the President of the United States
- ☐ Dance in the Mardi Gras parade in Rio

- ☐ Go to a prize fight in Vegas
- ☐ Take a Jell-O bath
- ☐ Follow the Oregon Trail in true pioneer fashion
- ☐ Sunbathe topless
- ☐ Reach Nirvana
- ☐ Be a game show contestant
- ☐ Solve a Mystery Train Ride
- ☐ Start an outrageous shoe collection
- ☐ Become an über-something
- ☐ Learn all the rules of football
- ☐ Learn to tell time by looking at the skies or paying attention to tides
- ☐ Do the I Ching

- [ ] Live communally
- [ ] Enjoy the frozen hot chocolate at Serendipity
- [ ] Have Beluga caviar, Nova Scotia smoked salmon, and Russian vodka for dinner
- [ ] Go on an open casting call
- [ ] Be a roadie
- [ ] Walk over hot coals
- [ ] Become a dual citizen
- [ ] Reverse a Supreme Court Decision
- [ ] Camp in the Chukot region of Siberia
- [ ] Give every man thine ear, but few thy voice
- [ ] Carpool more

- [ ] Lobby for more women on U.S. currency

- [ ] Be a host for a foreign exchange student

- [ ] Carry on an intellectual conversation with the Dalai Lama

> *Consistency is the last refuge of the unimaginative.*
>
> —*Oscar Wilde*

- [ ] Say "Voulez-vous couchez avec moi?" to Gerard Depardieu

- [ ] Do shots with a Russian diplomat

- [ ] Trade jokes with Mel Brooks or Dana Carvey

☐ Caddy for Tiger Woods

☐ Sample the prune chili at Yuba City's annual California Prune Festival

☐ Host a game show

☐ Develop a new game show

☐ Invent an environmentally harmless mode of transportation

☐ Paint a masterpiece

☐ Put down the toilet seat

☐ Solve Rubik's Cube

☐ Get in touch with your inner adult

☐ Be on "Sesame Street"

☐ Paint your mailbox purple

☐ Try working at odd jobs like a weed farmer or a worm picker

- ☐ Go to Hell, Michigan, or enjoy Intercourse, Pennsylvania

- ☐ Be pictured on the front page of *The New York Times*

- ☐ Cross Ireland by bike

- ☐ Write an op ed piece for a major metropolitan daily

- ☐ Have your suit made to order by a top-notch tailor

- ☐ Create your own fragrance

- ☐ Distinguish the differences between Ionic, Corinthian, and Doric

- ☐ Attend the Governor's Inaugural Ball

- ☐ Arrive at church in a white stretch limousine

- [ ] Ride with the AmTrak engineer straight through the Rockies

- [ ] Stand on your head

- [ ] Be photographed by Annie Leibovitz, Herb Ritts, or Richard Avedon

- [ ] Publish your poem in the *New Yorker*

> *Life is half spent before one knows what life is.*
>
> —*French proverb*

- [ ] Take a month of weekends

- [ ] Execute a flawless triple axel

- [ ] Persuade your boss that a four-day weekend will result in more productivity

- ☐ Be nominated for a Pulitzer Prize

- ☐ Go back to where you came from

- ☐ Attend a tailgate party

- ☐ Have an imaginatively stocked picnic hamper

- ☐ Test drive all the new cars

- ☐ Have your milk delivered by a milkman

- ☐ Do time at a soup kitchen

- ☐ Be interviewed on a Barbara Walters' Special

- ☐ Give sex advice to Dr. Ruth

- ☐ Send in your Publisher's Clearing House entry

- ☐ Have your home drawn in charcoal and framed

- [ ] Wear flowers in your hair or lapels
- [ ] Get a free health club membership
- [ ] Spoil kids every once in a while
- [ ] Be extravagant with your praise
- [ ] Be a groupie
- [ ] Win with a royal flush
- [ ] Earn royalties
- [ ] Straighten George Steinbrenner out
- [ ] Down an imperial pint in London's Samuel Pepys pub on the Thames
- [ ] Grow your own vegetables
- [ ] Finish a Middleton acrostic in less than thirty minutes
- [ ] Get used to bifocals

- ☐ Know the difference between a Tee and a Hex nut, a Phillips and a slotted screw

- ☐ Operate a radial arm saw

- ☐ Shave with Kiehl's

- ☐ Make a wish upon a star

- ☐ Tour Slimbridge with Prince Charles

- ☐ Start at Lake Tear of the Clouds and go by canoe down the Hudson to the Statue of Liberty

- ☐ Have a secret hiding place

- ☐ Develop a list of graceful excuses for all those occasions you'd like to skip

- ☐ Have a best friend who's really honest when you need it

- ☐ Own a handknit sweater

- ☐ Let your hair down

- ☐ Wear a milk mustache in a "Got Milk?" ad, or be in a Waterman Pen ad

- ☐ Grow your nails long and be a hand model

- ☐ Make soup from scratch

- ☐ Revisit your first dorm room with your freshman roommate

- ☐ Know what you would be willing to do for a million dollars

- ☐ Have a sandwich, drink, or ice cream flavor named after you

- ☐ Buy a knighthood

- ☐ Watch the sunrise at Chichén Itzá

- ☐ Channel Hendrix or Lennon

Life is better than death,
I believe,
if only because
it is less boring,
and because it has
fresh peaches in it.

—Alice Walker

> *Life begets life. Energy creates energy. It is by spending oneself that one becomes rich.*
>
> —*Sarah Bernhardt*

- [ ] Know six things you would do if you were president

- [ ] Thank everyone

- [ ] Discourage all things that come in gray

- [ ] Stay at the Awani Hotel in Yosemite

- [ ] Know the three types of rocks

- [ ] Have great-great-grandchildren

- [ ] Daydream about what you would eat for your last meal and then eat it

☐ Solve the mystery of where Jimmy Hoffa was laid to rest

☐ Learn the names of the seven films in which John Wayne dies

☐ Listen to a whole week of Rush Limbaugh

☐ Play Blanche du Bois

☐ Watch *Bela Lugosi Meets a Brooklyn Gorilla* or *Devil Girls From Mars*

☐ Examine the *Titanic* wreck on the ocean floor

☐ Pilot the space shuttle

☐ Visit another planet

☐ Attend a presidential debate

☐ Play the didgeridoo or the hammered dulcimer

- [ ] Perfect your calligraphy
- [ ] Be a cryptographer
- [ ] Give credit where credit is due
- [ ] Be accountable
- [ ] Own a spacesuit
- [ ] Use a divining rod
- [ ] Perform an exorcism
- [ ] Have chocolate con churros after an all-nighter in Barcelona
- [ ] Own a pit bull
- [ ] Know your senators
- [ ] Play Nora in *A Doll's House*
- [ ] Construct a card house
- [ ] Erect a statue

- [ ] Build a people pyramid

- [ ] Sing back-up

- [ ] Ballroom-dance at the Rainbow Room

- [ ] Bicycle through Bordeaux

- [ ] Mime for money

- [ ] Attend the Blessing of the Animals at New York City's Cathedral of St. John the Divine 🐕🐈🐕🐓🐇🐢🐖

- [ ] Claim you were on the Beatles' *Sergeant Pepper* album

- [ ] Harmonize "The Star Spangled Banner"

- [ ] Become a beer connoisseur

- [ ] Hire an escort

- [ ] Kiss women's hands

- ☐ Cure depression
- ☐ Define your utopia
- ☐ Be a best boy
- ☐ Be intimate with _____
- ☐ Be a most valuable player

> *He who hesitates is a damn fool.*
>
> —*Mae West*

- ☐ Know what a key grip does
- ☐ Be radiant
- ☐ Run through a carwash
- ☐ Deliver a baby
- ☐ Adopt a baby

- ☐ Study Stanislavski
- ☐ Tame lions
- ☐ See a quetzal in the wild
- ☐ Discover a new species in the rain forest canopy
- ☐ Be in *The Guinness Book of World Records*
- ☐ Drink a pint of Guinness
- ☐ Get on the guest list
- ☐ Study war
- ☐ Defrost the freezer
- ☐ Study war no more
- ☐ Be truly color-blind
- ☐ Know what syzygy is

- [ ] Have great friends
- [ ] Have friends in high places
- [ ] Have friends in low places
- [ ] Have friends from all parts of your life
- [ ] Cultivate grace
- [ ] Exercise restraint
- [ ] Create a computer program
- [ ] Freefall with an umbrella
- [ ] End terrorism
- [ ] Patent a gene
- [ ] See the terra-cotta soldiers at Xian
- [ ] Be a freedom-fighter
- [ ] Join a manhunt, search party, or posse
- [ ] Sketch with your eyes closed

☐ Play the triangle or kazoo

☐ Eat a ripe mango

☐ Ride every roller coaster in the continental United States

☐ Own a pair of chaps

☐ Be a smokejumper

☐ Master a Billy Wilder, David Mamet, or Tarantinian dialogue

☐ Tour a brewery

☐ Eat a four-pound steak

☐ Savor the spotlight

☐ Ride in a sidecar

☐ Hunt for breakfast

☐ Recognize auras and chakras

☐ Witness a death

☐ Make your parents and children teary with pride

☐ Play spin the bottle

☐ Study witchcraft

☐ Be a centerfold

☐ Replace all your records with CDs

☐ Replace all your CDs with records

☐ Yearn

☐ Write a children's story

☐ Swan-dive into a crowd that is prepared to catch you

☐ Give everyone you love a note outlining how they've enriched your life

☐ Speak your piece

☐ Speak your peace

> *If I had to live my life again, I'd make the same mistakes, only sooner.*
>
> —Tallulah Bankhead

☐ Ring a really big bell

☐ Act with the courage of your convictions

☐ Laugh until you're dizzy

☐ Tour the Prado, the Louvre, the Hermitage, the Metropolitan, and the Uffizi

☐ Have outercourse

☐ Take a self-defense course

☐ Discover a planet

- [ ] Eat a fish boil in Door County, Wisconsin

- [ ] Read aloud *Alexander and the Terrible, Horrible, No Good, Very Bad Day*

- [ ] Fit twelve friends into a phone booth or a Beetle

- [ ] Own some go-go boots

- [ ] Have a virtual affair

- [ ] Turn off the television and go look at the stars

- [ ] Squeeze a glass of fresh orange juice

- [ ] Teach the dog to bring in the paper

- [ ] Acquire meaningful Christmas ornaments

- [ ] Draw up a living will

☐ Eat less fat

☐ Eat more fat

☐ Free a political prisoner

☐ Cuddle infants with AIDS

☐ Volunteer at a cancer ward

☐ Save your soul

☐ Buy this book

☐ Count up everything in these pages
   you've already done

☐ Have one original thought

☐ Contribute to world peace

☐ Live